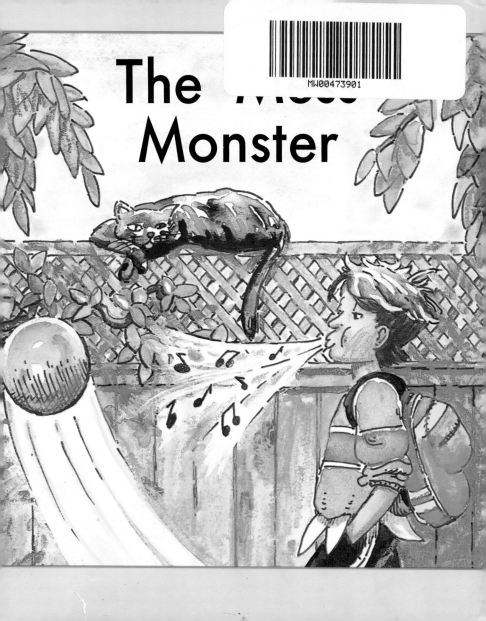

The Mess
Monster

When Samson got home,
he dumped his ball
in the corner of his bedroom.

"Pick it up, Samson," said Dad.
But Samson didn't.

When Samson got ready
for his bath,
he dumped his clothes
in the corner of his bedroom
on top of his ball.

"Pick them up, Samson,"
said Dad.
But Samson didn't.

4

Before he went to bed,
Samson played a game
with his big sister, Ellen.

Samson dumped the game
in the corner of his bedroom
on top of his clothes and his ball.

"Pick it up, Samson," said Ellen.
But Samson didn't.

When Samson was in bed,
his big brother, George,
read him a book
about a monster.

Samson dumped the book
in the corner of his bedroom
on top of the game, his clothes,
and his ball.

"Pick it up, Samson,"
said George.
But Samson didn't.

In the middle of the night,
Samson woke up.
He saw a monster
in the corner of his bedroom.
"Help! Help!" he screamed.

Dad turned on the light,
and this is what Samson saw...